Samuel French Acting Edition

I Used To Write On Walls

by Bekah Brunstetter

SAMUELFRENCH.COM SAMUELFRENCH.CO.UK

Copyright © 2008 by Bekah Brunstetter
All Rights Reserved

I USED TO WRITE ON WALLS is fully protected under the copyright laws of the United States of America, the British Commonwealth, including Canada, and all other countries of the Copyright Union. All rights, including professional and amateur stage productions, recitation, lecturing, public reading, motion picture, radio broadcasting, television and the rights of translation into foreign languages are strictly reserved.

ISBN 978-0-573-65143-4

www.SamuelFrench.com
www.SamuelFrench.co.uk

FOR PRODUCTION ENQUIRIES

UNITED STATES AND CANADA
Info@SamuelFrench.com
1-866-598-8449

UNITED KINGDOM AND EUROPE
Plays@SamuelFrench.co.uk
020-7255-4302

Each title is subject to availability from Samuel French, depending upon country of performance. Please be aware that *I USED TO WRITE ON WALLS* may not be licensed by Samuel French in your territory. Professional and amateur producers should contact the nearest Samuel French office or licensing partner to verify availability.

CAUTION: Professional and amateur producers are hereby warned that *I USED TO WRITE ON WALLS* is subject to a licensing fee. Publication of this play(s) does not imply availability for performance. Both amateurs and professionals considering a production are strongly advised to apply to Samuel French before starting rehearsals, advertising, or booking a theatre. A licensing fee must be paid whether the title(s) is presented for charity or gain and whether or not admission is charged. Professional/Stock licensing fees are quoted upon application to Samuel French.

No one shall make any changes in this title(s) for the purpose of production. No part of this book may be reproduced, stored in a retrieval system, or transmitted in any form, by any means, now known or yet to be invented, including mechanical, electronic, photocopying, recording, videotaping, or otherwise, without the prior written permission of the publisher. No one shall upload this title(s), or part of this title(s), to any social media websites.

For all enquiries regarding motion picture, television, and other media rights, please contact Samuel French.

MUSIC USE NOTE

Licensees are solely responsible for obtaining formal written permission from copyright owners to use copyrighted music in the performance of this play and are strongly cautioned to do so. If no such permission is obtained by the licensee, then the licensee must use only original music that the licensee owns and controls. Licensees are solely responsible and liable for all music clearances and shall indemnify the copyright owners of the play(s) and their licensing agent, Samuel French, against any costs, expenses, losses and liabilities arising from the use of music by licensees. Please contact the appropriate music licensing authority in your territory for the rights to any incidental music.

IMPORTANT BILLING AND CREDIT REQUIREMENTS

If you have obtained performance rights to this title, please refer to your licensing agreement for important billing and credit requirements.

I USED TO WRITE ON WALLS was first produced by Working Man's Clothes Productions at the Gene Frankel Undeground, NYC, October 2008. The directors were Diana Basmajian and Isaac Byrne, produced by Jared Culverhouse, lighting design by Jake Platt, Set design by April Barlett, original music composition by Randy Garcia, Costumes by Candace Thompson, production managed by Will Neuman, and was stage managed by Jenna Dempsey. The cast was as follows:

TREVOR	Jeff Berg
DIANE	Maggie Hamilton
JOANNE	Darcie Champagne
GEORGIA	Lavita Shaurice
MONA	Ellen David
ANNA	Chelsey Shannon
ANNA'S MOTHER	Rachel Dorfman
DIANE'S MOTHER	Mary Round

CHARACTERS

THE BOY:

TREVOR, 24. Sexy. Oh my God. Sexy. Stoned, oblivious. Philosopher, Surfer, Skater.

THE LADIES:

MOM, 30 and 55. She wishes Everything for You, even if you don't wish it for Yourself. She is not as Pretty as she once was. (Can be double cast, or played as separate characters).

ANNA, 11. Silly Snow White beautiful. You can't help but Stare.

DIANE, 34. A cop. Just a trace of pretty. At That Breaking Point of Aloneliness.

MONA, 40. An Astronaut who Also Quilts.

JOANNE, 30. Make-up Expert. Go see her on the Second Floor. She's always there.

GEORGIA, 23. Beat poet. Dark, frightening prettiness; but a big, awkward nose.

TIME/PLACE

Now; the Big City.

STAGE

A large brick wall. The city behind it. Behind that, the moon.

ACT I

Prologue

(A backyard. In it: **ANNA**, *11, beautiful. She plays the harp. She's also got a red popsicle. She sings as she plays. She's not bad.)*

ANNA. Happy Eleventth birthday to me, happy 'leventh birthday to me.

Happy Birthday to Anna, Happy Birthday to me!

(A motherish voice, from across the yard. We don't see her.)

MOM. ANNA! IT'S TIME TO COME INSIDE!
ANNA. IN A MINUTE! I'M BUSY!

(She resumes singing, playing.)

Next year you'll be twelve, Next year you'll be twelve! Gonna shed your pla-cent-a, next year you'll be twelve!

(She looks down at her lap. It's got some red on it. She jumps up.)

MOM! MOM! MOM! MOM! MOM!

MOM. *(cheerful and Birthday, O.S.)* What, Beautiful?
ANNA. I GOT MY PERIOD! I GOT MY PERIOD! I'M ON THE RAG!

(**MOM** *enters, weary. Whoa. Not as pretty as* **ANNA**. **MOM** *inspects.*)

MOM. No, Sweetie, you just dropped your popsicle on your lap.

ANNA. ...Oh. (*Pause.*) I want it. I'm tired of *waiting* I've been waiting my whole life since I was *born.*

MOM. I know, honey, but you have to be P – (**ANNA** *looks directly at her mother. This hurts.*)

Ow. Honey, please don't look directly at me. It stings.

(**ANNA** *adverts her gaze.*)

Now, come on. It's time to come in. Your cousin's picking you up in ten minutes. Bring your harp inside and put on the special dress.

ANNA. That dress makes my titties look small!

MOM. You don't *have* any –

(**ANNA** *sticks out her chest. They're sprouting, yes.*)

Wow. Right. Well. Already. Where did those come from?

ANNA. I don't know, maybe heaven.

MOM. When I was your age, I – like a – I *prayed* for mine to happen, I mean, ON MY KNEES, and I didn't even believe in *God.*

Except for when I wanted something. Hmm. I guess that's still the same. I guess I'm still a girl.

But I was definitely no younger than thirteen when I – when they – and they STILL weren't THAT –

(*She looks her own breasts, then back at* **ANNA**.)

There they are. Already. I bet they're going to be big. Someone's going to make a home between them.

Someone's going to pitch a tent.

ANNA. Where's he taking me?

MOM. To the beach.

ANNA. I don't wanna go to the beach.

MOM. Anna – Don't start. Your cousin's moving in a few days and this is the last chance you're going to get to spend time with him before he goes. He wants to take you to the beach for your birthday, isn't that nice?

ANNA. But I wanna go to Sarah's! She's says I could come over and she wants to do my hair like Cameron Diaz. It's my special day!

MOM. Your cousin is taking you to the *beach* and that's that. Any girl your age would be lucky to spend an afternoon with a guy like him.

ANNA. Ew. Mom.

MOM. That's not what I – (*Pause.*) Hmmm. Maybe I – maybe that is what I meant.

ANNA. Just cause Aunt Brooke shot herself doesn't mean I have to do whatever he wants me to do. If you shot yourself, I would not use that as an excuse to get what I want.

(*Pause.*)

MOM. I liked you better when you didn't have your own thoughts.

ANNA. When was that?

MOM. When you were small.

ANNA. I'm still small. I was small yesterday.

MOM. When you were super small and still smelled like me.

ANNA. Whenever we go in his car he plays his music too

loud. And his cigarettes smell funny. And last time in the car he farted and didn't say excuse me and then he looked at me like he was looking at a cookie. I'm bored of people looking at me all the time.

(*Pause.*)

MOM. Do You know how pretty you are?

ANNA. I guess.

MOM. Honey, you make people stare. The other day at the grocery store you made a man drop a whole watermelon. You make people trip over things and walk into stationary objects. I need you to appreciate this. Not everyone is as fortunate as you.

ANNA. Like who?

MOM. Well. Me.

ANNA. You're very cute.

MOM. Thank you.

ANNA. You're welcome.

MOM. God. What I would've given at your age to have a face like yours.

ANNA. You can have it. I don't need it.

MOM. Really? Are you sure? Because Sometimes I really do wish I could borrow it, or just parts. Your eyes, your skin. Your lips, your white teeth. The way your lips suggest your teeth – like your teeth are the dirty secret of your mouth.

ANNA. Oh.

MOM. You're so pretty you make your own mother want to shoplift the important parts of your face. But – but bring them right back, of course, just – borrow. For dates, and, so that – people will look, and – God, when

I look at you, when I try to make a point – I *ramble*. Listen to me.

I get lost in your face.

ANNA. (*innocently*) I'm so pretty that Dad left.

(*Pause. That stung. Let it sting.*)

MOM. Well, that's certainly an – interesting way to –

ANNA. That's what you told Aunt Brooke. I wasn't listening but I was.

MOM. Your father left because – *not* because –

(**ANNA** *feels something. She gasps. She holds up her hand for her mother to stop speaking. She looks up her dress, then back, disappointed.*)

ANNA. Nevermind. I thought I felt – Hey what does it feel like, anyways? The lady business, the first time, and after?

MOM. Your face – your body – your whole self – is going to literally *explode* with pretty.

ANNA. Does that hurt?

MOM. No, it's wonderful. Actually, I wouldn't know. Mine was more of a thud.

ANNA. And what else? What else happens?

MOM. …Things start to grow.

ANNA. Flowers?

MOM. Sure. Every room you have ever entered immediately fills with flowers. Or at least, this is how it feels.

ANNA. Purple flowers that smell like candy corn? Little white flowers the kind that float in dishes and tap water? The kind that float?

(*Pause.*)

MOM. You bet.

ANNA. That's what it feels like? For serious?

MOM. It's similar to – falling love. But you don't know that yet. But you will. Probably about 17,000 times. But when someone falls in love with *you* – that is – that is more of a secret red flower hiding in somebody's coat. One time I thought I felt it, but I was wrong. You, Anna, you'll feel it a million times. You better get used to it.

They'll be stuck in your hair.

ANNA. Sounds annoying. I like my *own* hair.

MOM. Ow. Stop looking at me. Don't look directly at me. It burns.

ANNA. Why?

MOM. It makes me sad. Close your eyes.

(**ANNA** *does so* **MOM** *can look at her face.*)

I still don't understand how your face happened. How it came out of mine.

ANNA. You are very clever and you have a very cute nose. Also, your eyes, too close together or not, are *very* nice.

(*Pause.*)

MOM. Come inside, *now*.

ANNA. I wanna stay out HERE. You just want me out of your hair so you can go play putt-putt with Larry.

MOM. I DESERVE TO FEEL PRETTY TOO.

ANNA. But you don't even LIKE him that much, you think the sex is okay good but you wish he'd hold you after and not excuse himself to the bathroom and stop looking at your face like he did before he undid your bra with his teeth. He does not give the best head ever but it's okay good. (*Pause.*)

And you wish that someone would have taught him the alphabet trick so that you could see more colors and more heaven when you come.

(**MOM** *just stares.*)

I was listening but I wasn't. Larry is not too attractive. I don't like how he stares at me, or how he smells like a Vienna sausage, or how much he stares at me. None of those things are good.

MOM. He does not – he does not stare at you. He stares at everything. Including *me*. Just the other day – he looked at me.

ANNA. (*quietly*) I believe you.

MOM. He's just very *observant*. He does not – he does *not* – stare at you.

ANNA. Yes he does. (*Pause.*)

MOM. Okay, Well maybe he does. (*Pause.*) Maybe a little. And – well – and besides, That is none of your – okay. Wow. / Anna –

ANNA. What's a placenta?

MOM. Okay. Anna? Inside, now.

ANNA. Tell me happy birthday first!

MOM. Happy Birthday first.

ANNA. Can I wear shorts?

MOM. Yes. Fine.

(**MOM** *starts to exit.*)

ANNA. Short short short ones?

MOM. Medium. Shorts that cover your business.
ANNA. Can I wear lip gloss?
MOM. No.

(Long pause. ANNA just sits. MOM is gone.)

MOM. *(O.S.)* Fine.

(ANNA *smiles. She stands up.)*

ANNA. I'm coming!

(She begins to drag her harp across the yard. it takes a while. While this happens, the wall is illuminated.)

I.

A big city. A brick wall. **TREVOR**, *24, is facing it, holding a can of kid's sidewalk chalk. Next to him, a beat up skateboard with a skull on the back. He's not wearing a shirt. He's lean, tan, and muscular, but in a soft boyish way. He inspects the wall. He moves his body in weird ways like he's trying to get inside of the brick. He listens to the brick. He smells the brick. He steps back. He thinks.*

DIANE, *34, a cop, enters. She stands guard. She does not notice* **TREVOR**, *at first. She radios in a report.*

DIANE. (*radio-ing, mildly bored, but official*) This is officer Wright, reporting from Guard base sector 8, 9:13 am, maintaining surveillance, rear entrance, all things clear, over.

She looks out, official. Few beats. She takes out her phone and stares at it. She stops. Nerves. She decides to make the call. It rings. Few Rings.

DIANE. Uh, *hey*, Ted, How are – (*Pause.*) Oh, that's – not you. That's your voicemail. Right. I was wondering why you sounded like a robot. No, I don't mean you sound like a robot. But if you did, that'd be okay. I'd still like you.

I guess I just admitted that I like you. I like you. I can say that. I like you. And I guess I did just say it. Three times.

So, um, hi, it was really nice to meet you the other night, we met at the – oh. Right. This is Diane. Diane Wright. Mrs. *Wright*. A-Ha. Ha. Right.

So it's Sunday, Sunday the 4th – at about um. 9 am. (*Pause.*) I'm sorry but I really don't know what I'm doing calling you or calling anyone at 9 am on a Sunday. You're probably at *church* – ha – no, I'm kidding – no, but, yeah, it'd be fine if you *were* at church, I don't mean to joke. Church is a very serious thing. Very. I myself just got sort of turned *off* to it in like seventh grade when I had this raging crush on my Sunday School teacher and he had an adulterous affair with the organ player, they were apparently caught having butt sex, I was devastated. (*Pause.*) I think I meant to say anal. Sex. (*Pause.*)

Yeah – so – this is Diane. It was really nice to meet you, I think that's the gist of – yeah – oh man, was I DRUNK! Merlot does this – thing – to my forehead – and to my pants – they fly off like – wow – yeah.

(*She laughs. She stops. Longish pause.*)

Um. I'd like to make dinner for you. A casserole. I make this thing that my Mom used to make – it's got chicken and rice and broccoli, and it's sort of creamy, cause there's cream of mushroom soup, and – well – I guess it's more of a BAKE than – I'm very free this week. I wanted to – what I meant to say was – what I wanted to say – I'm really lonely. I think that you are, too. Last night I woke up and I was – I was holding my pillow like somebody might hold someone they love. And I've been having these dreams that I give birth to whole people. Big sized ones. They come out smarter than me. They can name all fifty states and the rivers that run through them. (*Pause.*) I'm free all week. C-Call me.

(She starts to hang up.)

Thanks for the sex.

(She hangs up, Hating herself.)

Talk to you never.

Finally, She sees **TREVOR**. *In a cop like way, she watches him, suspiciously. He bends over to inspect more brick. She likes it.*

She can't help it. Any woman couldn't. He is just that hot.

Oh man.

He chooses a piece of water-blue chalk, and just before he starts to draw, **DIANE** *approaches.*

DIANE. *(power trip)* How you doing today?

TREVOR. Good.

DIANE. Nice day. Nice and bright.

TREVOR. Yeah, and the sun is real shiny, too.

DIANE. You going to write on that wall?

TREVOR. Nah, yeah, I was thinking about it.

(Pause.)

DIANE. Something profane?

(Pause. **TREVOR** *does not know what this word means.)*

It's my wall.

TREVOR. No *way.*

DIANE. Sort of. It's my duty to protect it. This building is vulnerable, see. I keep an eye out for suspicious activity. *(Pause.)* I'm in charge.

(**TREVOR** *gives a knowing nod.*)

What were you going to draw?

TREVOR. A sick ass wave. The most epic wave ever surfed.

(**TREVOR** *looks at the wall, envisioning the most epic wave ever surfed.*)

DIANE. That your chalk? It's kid's chalk.

TREVOR. It just washes away.

DIANE. Then why waste your time?

(**TREVOR** *shrugs. His shrug turns into a smile. He's the kind of guy who gets comfortable around strangers real fast.*)

TREVOR. You going to stop me?

DIANE. I haven't decided yet.

TREVOR. I'm not hurting anybody.

DIANE. I guess not.

TREVOR. So it's cool?

(**DIANE** *thinks.*)

DIANE. Uh –

(*He looks at her, for real. He smiles, irresistible, and she melts. We watch her melt.*)

Uh – Sure. Why not. But If – if I see another cop, I gotta pretend like I'm mad at you.

TREVOR. What are you, some kinda cop?

DIANE. Yeah…..I'm a cop. What, You surf?

TREVOR. Yeah.

DIANE. You like danger?

TREVOR. Nah.

DIANE. Risking your neck for a joyride. That's how it looks to me. Surfing, I mean. Gives you a good body, though. I mean, uh, wow, I mean, I mean the – muscles – involved in – engaged in –

(**DIANE** *makes a paddling motion.*)

Right. The muscles that – right. That's what I meant, when I said that, when I said that thing about you having a good body, I mean, surfers having good bodies. Generally. In general.

TREVOR. Nah. Those are big wave surfers, the guys with the big ass muscles, all ripped. Mine are alright. Those guys, THOSE guys are fucking nuts. I don't do that shit. I just do baby waves. I don't wanna *die* dude.

DIANE. Well, you could die right here, too.

TREVOR. Nah. Really?

(**DIANE** *points out beyond the street.*)

DIANE. See that building? It could fall.

TREVOR. Why would it fall?

DIANE. Why not, if it wanted to? And see that truck? Driver could fall asleep. Plow right into you. Smush you against your palate.

TREVOR. Nah, man, Id jump outta the way.

DIANE. You wouldn't be fast enough. No one's ever fast enough to jump outta the way of their own death.

It's crazy. Yeah, I've seen it all.

There's enough crazy stuff, I seen it, there's enough going down to keep one from wanting to go out in the ocean – a very powerful thing, mind you – on some flimsy *board* and create it. (*Pause*) That's what I think about it, about danger and chasing it and stuff.

TREVOR. Yeah, sometimes I don't think I'll live my whole life. Sometimes I wake up and think today – I'm going to die. But it hasn't happened yet or anything.

DIANE. What do you do about feeling like you're gonna die?

TREVOR. Say a Prayer. Or forget about it.

DIANE. You pray?

TREVOR. Hell yeah, I love church. It's so rad. Good stories. Good people. Old ladies with cool hats. The other day God knew how bad I wanted a taco, and he said to me, I'm going to take you to get the best taco of your life. And you know what? He did.

(**TREVOR** *gives a weird, knowing nod. This charms* **DIANE**.)

DIANE. So, uh – are you gonna draw the wave or not?

TREVOR. You're not gonna stop me?

(**DIANE** *shakes her head. He starts to draw. He takes it SO seriously. He puts his body inside the shape, closes his eye, trying to precisely remember the most epic wave ever. This goes on for a minute and she watches.*)

DIANE. I used to write on walls.

(*He doesn't respond. Neither are listening to each other.*)

Back when I was a punk kid.

TREVOR. I'm not a punk. Well punk rock, hell yeah.

DIANE. I'm just saying I understand what you're doing.

(**TREVOR** *takes a step back, examines the wave, which is beginning to take shape. It is nothing special.*)

TREVOR. So, like, what do you think?

DIANE. It's alright. Looks like a wave to me.

TREVOR. No, see, that's where it breaks. That's right where you have to ride it. Right there.

(*He puts himself inside of it. He speaks with intense pride and enthusiasm.*)

See, you gotta, fuckin, you gotta BE there. You gotta be ready for it, you gotta be right there feeling that break and reading its mind or you're fucked, you're either washed up bored or fucked. Hell yeah. But then you try again.

DIANE. I see. I guess.

TREVOR. Yeah, I'm not very good at drawing, so.

DIANE. What'd you come to the city for if you wanna surf so bad?

TREVOR. See, I'm on this like, rad, rad philosophical journey. The journey needed me here.

DIANE. What kind of journey?

TREVOR. I'm going to solve all the problems in the world. One by one. But first I'm taking this philosophy class at this school thing. It's so rad. We like read and then talk about the stuff we read.

(**DIANE** *smiles.*)

And Plus there's good places to surf here. Hour North. I can't figure out how to get there yet, I haven't figured it out. I'll figure it out.

DIANE. The train?

TREVOR. Huh? Oh. Yeah.

(**DIANE** *notices another cop. She snaps to attention.*

TREVOR *does not see the cop. Her demeanor instantly changes. She addresses* **TREVOR**.)

Listen you – Sir – I need you to back away from the wall, sir. Drop the chalk and back away from the wall.

TREVOR. Huh?

DIANE. Defacing public property, sir, is an offense. This public property was not erected for you to go willy nilly upon it with your chalk. PLEASE BACK AWAY FROM THE WALL.

(**DIANE** *looks. The cop is gone. Her demeanor changes again.*)

Sorry. Po Po.

(**TREVOR** *really looks at her for the first time.*)

TREVOR. That was kinda hot.

DIANE. Uh – what?

TREVOR. Wow, what's your name?

DIANE. Diane.

TREVOR. Wow, Diane, you're pretty rad for a cop.

DIANE. Thank you.

TREVOR. And wow, you have beautiful eyes. I mean, BEAUTIFUL. You should like, be in a car commercial. Like saying, *hey, buy this car cause I'm pretty.*

DIANE. (*seriously blushing.*) Oh come on.

TREVOR. No, you are like, really rad for a cop. Do you have kids?

DIANE. No.

(**TREVOR** *smiles at her, nodding.* **DIANE** *can't help but smile back. This whole thing seems ridiculous. Did he really just call her pretty?*)

TREVOR. Oh man. I want some pizza.

DIANE. I like pizza, too.

TREVOR. Fuck yeah, pizza. With like, lots of stuff on it. Tons of stuff.

DIANE. But no mushrooms.

TREVOR. *Fuck* mushrooms.

DIANE. Yeah, I agree.

TREVOR. I'm Trevor.

(He extends his hand. They shake like buddies.)

Whoa, you shake just like my buddy! I got this buddy Graham back in Cali, we got this Tshirt company together? I make these rad designs with like um DRAGONS and SKULLS and WAVES and he puts words on them like RAD and SICK and you shake just like him.

DIANE. Th – thank you.

TREVOR. It's a pleasure to meet you, beautiful lady.

DIANE. You're kidding, right?

TREVOR. What?

DIANE. This whole, thing. You're kidding. I'm a cop. You're kidding.

TREVOR. No. You're a beautiful lady, beautiful lady.

*(Long pause. **DIANE** is stunned.)*

DIANE. Uh – Th – Thank you.

*(**TREVOR** is confused by the look of awkward terror on her face.)*

TREVOR. Whoa – are you gonna puke?

DIANE. I'm sorry. I'm sorry. This has just, um, this has never happened to me. I've been waiting since I got my first p – I mean, since, uh – since like seventh grade for this to happen to me. For somebody to – for a stranger to – find me – to tell me I'm – and I don't mean homeless people or like, people with strollers full of old lettuce – I mean, an actual person.

(**TREVOR** *gets up and puts his shirt back on.* **DIANE** *watches. Goodbye, beautiful body. There it goes.*)

TREVOR. Thanks for letting me draw my sick wave.

DIANE. *Sure.* It was fun. For me too. I mean, you know. To watch. Not you. But it. Yeah. It reminded me of when. Things I used to do. Ha. Things I don't do anymore.

(*He goes.* **DIANE** *thinks about going after him, then doesn't. He comes back.*)

TREVOR. Hey, uh, do you like, wanna talk about philosophy sometime?

DIANE. What?

TREVOR. Like, maybe get together over a coffee and talk about philosophy?

DIANE. I – guess.

TREVOR. (*taking out his phone*) What's your number?

DIANE. 546 6677.

(*He enters it.*)

TREVOR. Cool. Well. See you.

(*He starts to go.*)

DIANE. WAIT. That's not my number.

TREVOR. Uh.

DIANE. Sorry, I just. Can I just have yours, instead? I just. Checkered past. I'm a bit, run over. What I mean is

– when you were born, I was – I'm older than you. Probably. I'm thirty-four. Years old. That's my age.

(**TREVOR** *just stares at her.*)

Look, hey, I'm not proud of it.

TREVOR. (*smiling*) Age is like, crazy, you know? Ever think about it, man? Age is like the *thing* that we *are*. We *are* our *age* and it like keeps going up and up the metaphysical ladder of life and then we die.

(*He goes to the wall. He writes his number in chalk, inside the wave.*)

Nice meeting you, pretty lady.

He leaves on the skateboard, and we can hear it. It's how we can always know that he is coming or going: and it's hot.

She goes to his wave and touches it, attempts to ride it. She Copies down the number. Looks around, conscious of a few people passing by. She Clears her throat. Stands, erect. Looks out, official.

II.

A mike drops. in front of the wall. A club, the city, low-lit, sort of full, but no one's really paying attention to **GEORGIA** *as she takes the stage, petrified but powerful. She hesitates, clears her throat, performs.*

GEORGIA. You are listening to the words of
the white boy
who knocked you up, accidentally,
when you got drunk and bounced on his big dick
six Saturday's ago.
He has written a new beat and
it's really, really good.
Sort of.

But you lost it, so, there it went, in a way.
Peeing out what could have been was weird
and felt like a period,
like nothing, like something since seventh grade.
But it happened,
and when it did, what would have been your kid
left you with the rhythm of his words,
backed by beats that shake you now
with his not knowing.
What would have been but shouldn't (so good, I guess)
would have been white and talented and
quite the lady's man and a drinker
and a big thinker
and a soon to be baby daddy who knows nothing of it and
he woulda dropped albums like drunk compliments
in recording studios that wither and shake
with potential like
the walls of your stomach.

(*A few claps, but nothing much.* **GEORGIA** *bows, awkwardly.*)

GEORGIA. Thank you. Thank you. That was a little something I wrote for – a young man who (*she peers out into the crowd. Peers, hard.*) Right. He's not here. Right. Thanks for um – thanks.

(*She Walks off. Spot and mike are gone.*)

III.

The park. Birds, nice. **DIANE** *is off work, starring at the piece of paper. She looks at it, she puts it in her pocket. She takes it out, looks at it. Throws it. Looks at it. Picks it back up. Looks at it. Looks at it.*

JOANNE, *post-work, joins her on the opposite end of the bench. She is irksomely happy. This irks* **DIANE**. **JOANNE** *Applies make-up, strategically.* **DIANE** *throws the paper again.* **JOANNE** *notices, picks it up, hands it back to her.*

JOANNE. Here, you dropped this.

DIANE. No, I threw it.

JOANNE. Okay, well, here.

(**DIANE** *takes it back. She looks at it some more.* **JOANNE** *continues with her face but sneaks looks at* **DIANE**. *Long beat of this.*)

I'm sorry, but hi.

DIANE. Hi.

JOANNE. Hi. I don't usually do this.

DIANE. Do What?

JOANNE. Talk to people I don't know. It's just that I've recently discovered my self-confidence. (*She smiles.*) I met a boy. A guy. I mean a man- person.

I've learned to legitimately love my vagina. I used to hate it. I think it's the grossest thing, don't you? Like a hairy piece of cake. What? Yes. Okay and what you're doing with your eyes is doing nothing for them, way too dark.

DIANE. What?

JOANNE. Your eye make up, it's – redundant.

DIANE. Oh – um – oh.

JOANNE. See, your eyes are *already* dark. So what you're doing there, with the – with the insistent tracing of them with what – what is that – midnight blue?

DIANE. Plum. It's supposed to be plum.

JOANNE. I would *kill* to have such dark eyes. They look like a storm. (*She leans in closer, looks.*) See mine? Look. Mine suck. My eyes are the color of the grass underneath a small inflatable swimming pool at the end of the Summer. I wish they would die.

DIANE. That's very specific.

JOANNE. And – hmmm. You've got make-up lines. All Along your jaw. Remember that bitchy cheerleader in tenth grade we all wanted to bury alive in the baseball field, that girl. That's what it's like. A little. I'm sorry. It's like you've got one face on top of another, You're lying to yourself.

(*Pause.*)

About the color of your skin.

(*Pause.*)

I'd recommend something much lighter, something softer, something more Spring. Something more, I'm in Easter bonnet with all my frills upon it, and everything is all honey ham and daisies in a basket, something more like that.

DIANE. My mom always said I was a fall.

JOANNE. Honey. If you're a fall, then I'm a *winter*.

(*She laughs.*)

Did your mom tell you to wear coral, too? That's what mom's do. They want us to be hideous school teacher creatures so that they don't have to think about us having sex. May I?

DIANE. May you, may you what?

JOANNE. Just give me two minutes. I promise. You won't regret it.

(JOANNE *removes a fat make-up bag from her purse.*)

DIANE. I don't – um – I don't usually –

JOANNE. Exactly.

DIANE. Sure. Why not.

(JOANNE *scoots close to her and starts fixing her face.*)

JOANNE. So okay, what I'm going to do is do something soft. Then I'll show you how to pump it up for nighttime, okay? But the soft look you can wear *now*. For sitting in the park and unexpected trips to the gynecologist and for work.

This is going to do wonders. Even in the work place, with a softer, more feminine look, you have no idea what – what a *difference* it makes –

You'll see, you have no idea how many people I've fixed up that I hear later have gotten raises, promoted, pregnant, I mean, real results, what do you do?

DIANE. I'm a cop.

JOANNE. ...Oh. Well, still. You have the right to remain properly highlighted!

DIANE. Do I.

JOANNE. I mean it, you're going to see a real difference. Take me, for example.

I used to never wear make-up at all and then one day I saw a picture of myself and realized that I was ugly. It was then that I realized why people stared. I had convinced myself up until that point that it was because I was so beautiful.

Now I work hard for my trace of cute. I know my face.

DIANE. I bet if we were friends, if – I bet I would think you were beautiful.

JOANNE. Probably not. I'm very selfish. I have horrible flaws. This I didn't know until my ex-fiance figured it out. See, I don't have that radiant inner glow that compensates for – I'm not that kind of girl.

DIANE. Me Neither.

JOANNE. I also have low self esteem. I feel very man-like most of the time. See, I have three brothers and every time I look in the mirror I see one of them crawling around in my face. I wanted to feel like a girl again, so I decided to get into cosmetology. Just for myself, at first.

So I started doing some stuff here, accentuating there, and baddabing, I met my fiancé. It was a very lovely engagement.

DIANE. It didn't – ?

JOANNE. No. But I found my knack for color and a full-time job. So fuck that faggot in the ass and bury him out back, right? Put a gun to that fucker's balls and blow.

DIANE. ...Right.

JOANNE. Pout your lips.

(*She does so.*)

Just cause you're a cop doesn't mean your can't embrace your inner flora and fauna. Your je ne sais quoi. That means *I don't know what.* I looked it up. I typed it into a translator. BECAUSE: There a lot of things, things that – people just SAY – that we're all expected to know – and I never know. Like what does precocious MEAN even and how do you even spell it?

DIANE. I don't know either.

JOANNE. Close your eyes.

DIANE. I did an internet dating thing. I actually paid.

JOANNE. So bad. Awful. I was nearly raped, and not only that, but I think I liked it. Look up.

(**DIANE** *looks up.* **JOANNE** *lines her eyes.*)

DIANE. So you – I guess the game is – well – it's like a bar? But. It's lists and secrets, how people WISH they were, you know, like, *I'm really athletic and spiritual and I don't like carrots and here are the five best pictures of me in the world.*

Pictures that are like – Oh – *I don't see you, the camera,* but they totally do. They staged the whole thing. (*Pause.*) So I had my good pictures up there, whatever, or I tried. And then one time I met up with a guy from there and he showed up wasted and kept calling me Tabitha and threw up all over my new bathmat.

JOANNE. Your name's not Tabitha?

DIANE. No, it's Diane.

JOANNE. Joanne and Diane. I'm Joanne. That's cute. I like that. There's a word for that.

DIANE. And then there was, of course, the time the actor guy waited til I had him in my mouth to tell me he was married.

JOANNE. Wow – did you finish?
DIANE. I felt obliged.
JOANNE. Did / he
DIANE. In my hair.

(*JOANNE finishes.*)

JOANNE. There. Done.

(*JOANNE gets a little mirror for her to take a gander.*)

DIANE. (*looking, wowed.*) Wow....I look like *you*.
JOANNE. You like it?
DIANE. Wow. I've never –
JOANNE. You've never looked so *pretty!*
DIANE. I mean I haven't, I really haven't.
JOANNE. You like it?!
DIANE. I'm – sparkling.
JOANNE. It's the slight shimmer powder I lightly dusted along your jaw line.
DIANE. It's great.
JOANNE. You like it, you like it?!
DIANE. Yeah. I really do.
JOANNE. (*giving her a card*) Here you go, I'm always there and I'm always bored. Second floor.
DIANE. Thanks.
JOANNE. Sure thing. Well. Back to work. (*Getting her stuff together*) You should call him.
DIANE. Who?
JOANNE. The phone number. In your hand.
DIANE. Oh.
JOANNE. You should call him.

DIANE. He's gotta be some ten years younger than me. And a lot smarter I think.

JOANNE. Oh, well they give better head.

DIANE. Smarter or younger?

JOANNE. Both.

DIANE. Really?

JOANNE. Definitely. Call him.

DIANE. Maybe.

JOANNE. Is he hot?

(**DIANE** *blushes.*)

You should definitely at least make an attempt to tap it.

DIANE. I'm afraid we, I – (*She laughs.*) I would – never get out of bed. I would just want to spend the rest of my life running my fingers over his – Wow. Okay.

(*She's thinking about it. It's hot.*)

Oh my God. I'm too old for this.

JOANNE. (*Getting up to go, smiles.*) *Call* him.

DIANE. (*Smiles, too.*) Thanks.

(**JOANNE** *leaves.* **DIANE** *looks at the paper. Takes out her phone.*)

IV.

The exposed brick of an apartment. A bed. **JOANNE** *is surrounded by make-up.*

JOANNE. HEY! I'm not done yet – don't look, you said you wouldn't look, I'm not done! Are you done peeing yet? Are you having a good pee? I bet your pee smells like rose cigars! I bet it's like a little party!

(*Pause.* **JOANNE** *listens for her dude.*)

I've been thinking about my birthday and what we should do on it. No, we don't have to do anything. I don't want to. But if YOU want to. Whatever you do, DON'T surprise me with flowers at work, don't make people look at me and at the flowers you've surprised me with. Don't bring them in yourself with no shirt. On. Definitely don't do that. That sounds. That sounds. (*She smiles.*) Awful.

I dreamt last night I had to have surgery but there was no such thing as anesthesia! They were going to pull a bone out /through my –

(*A toilet flushes.* **TREVOR** *emerges, no shirt, half made up with make up. He's like a giant little boy.*)

You fall in?

TREVOR. Huh? Nah. I was just like thinking about ways to fix all the problems of the world and I forgot what I was doing. AND I forgot to wash my HANDS! They got PEE on them!!!

(*Like a giant little boy, he sticks pee hands on her face. She squeals, squirms*)

JOANNE. (laughing) No! NO NO NO!! Stop!

(*Eventually he stops, snickering.*)

Let me finish you, you're incomplete.

(*He settles. She begins to apply eye shadow.*)

You can be Liberal with the lighter shade under your brow because it makes your eyes look bigger.

(*Pause.* **TREVOR** *is still thinking about the word liberal.*)

TREVOR. Liberal. That's funny. Which one is that? Those are the ones that like, are for abortions and stuff. Fuck *that*.

JOANNE. What's wrong with abortions?

TREVOR. God doesn't like them. God, like, likes babies a lot and stuff and wants them to live. He wants them to, like, THRIVE and like GROW and like BE who they ARE and stuff and grow up to BE Who they ARE.

(*By now, he's probably standing on the bed. He looks at the wall.*)

JOANNE. I love you.

TREVOR. That brick wall is fucking sick. We should write on it.

JOANNE. Are you kidding? No. It'd never come off. I'd get charged a buttload. Come back and Pout your lips. Yeah.

(*She puts lip gloss on him*)

TREVOR. It's rad you know so much about make-up. Make-up is so crazy. It's like the thing – that girls – ladies – are NOT. It's like the – the opposite of what you are.

You know?

JOANNE. Definitely.

> (*She works. She studies him. She smiles, huge. Buries her face in a pillow with joy.*)

TREVOR. ...What?

JOANNE. I'm sorry, I just – I can't believe the way this has all – Look at you. In my apartment.
This whole thing. The way this has worked out, I, I'm so happy. Tell me if it's annoying.

TREVOR. Nah. Being happy is good.

JOANNE. See, Girls, women, we – wait. We wait for moments like – when you – when I was waiting for that train and you just came up to me like you always hope someone will and you said, remember what you said? Remember what it was about?

TREVOR. Nah.

JOANNE. It was the weather.

TREVOR. Cool.

JOANNE. And I'm just so glad you said it, because – It was the kind of moment that women wait for. Harder that death.

> (*Pause.* **TREVOR** *doesn't get it, but he nods like he does.*)

God – I wish you knew what it was like to be in bed with you.

TREVOR. (*dumbly, like a little boy*) I'm good?

JOANNE. There's nothing fucking about it. It's the softest – most wonderful thing. It's like having simultaneous sex with every guy from high school I was in love with who wouldn't give me the time of day, and after, they all give me flowers and compliments. It's almost like that, but sweatier.

TREVOR. There was a girl once I did for a while, made love to her I mean, whatever, she had a broken neck.

(*Pause.*)

Yeah she had fallen off a horse and broke her neck. She could barely move, I had to do her like that. Soft so I wouldn't hurt her.

(*And this is the most romantic thing she has ever heard.*)

JOANNE. Oh. That's.

TREVOR. Am I too loud? When I do it?

JOANNE. No, not – you're perfect. Just right. You're like a bunny on a loaf of white bread.

TREVOR. I got used to – in my Mom's house – I got used to having to be all quiet? She didn't like to listen to it. I like it better quiet.

JOANNE. Okay – Done.

(*She hands him a mirror. He inspects.*)

TREVOR. Whoa, I look gay.

JOANNE. No, you don't, you look pretty.

TREVOR. I'm not pretty, YOU'RE pretty.

JOANNE. Not as pretty as *you*.

TREVOR. Nuh UH.

(*They might wrestle, laugh, and then they definitely kiss.* **JOANNE** *eats up these kisses, they are the best kisses in the world. For* **TREVOR***, it's more of a kissing game.*)

JOANNE. Am I prettier than the prettiest girl you've ever dated?

JOANNE. Whoa, we're dating? I mean I thought we were just like – hanging out -

(**JOANNE** *is a bit hurt and taken aback, but tries to conceal this.*)

JOANNE. No – yeah- I was just wondering if – Okay, well then, whose the prettiest girl you've ever – you know. Who's the best?

(**TREVOR** *thinks. He thinks a lot. He gets lost.*)

TREVOR. What was the question?

JOANNE. The prettiest. The prettiest girl you've ever – And whether or not I'm –

TREVOR. Oh, yeah, well it was probably this one girl I knew. Nah, I don't know.

(*Pause.* **JOANNE** *tries not to show the falling of his face.*)

We didn't really like – date – or anything, there was just – stuff in the air.

JOANNE. I like that you're honest.

TREVOR. You wanna smoke?

JOANNE. Didn't we just do that?

(*It wasn't really a question. He pulls a joint out of his pocket and lights it. He moves to the window, blowing smoke out of it. He examines the city, and philosophically ponders the idea of them. This happens mainly in his eyebrows.*)

TREVOR. Cities are crazy. There need to be, like, more cities or like less of them.

(*Pause.* **JOANNE** *needs him closer, so she says this*)

JOANNE. I ran into George the other day.

TREVOR. Who?

JOANNE. George. My ex fiancé.

> (*Pause. She waits for this to hit him, but it doesn't. So she says this.*)

> Did I ever tell you he slept with my best friend? My then best friend. I think. While my Mom was dying. Yeah.

TREVOR. Whoa, Your Mom's dead?

JOANNE. Yeah.

TREVOR. Mine too.

> (*Pause. They look at each other. They make out.* **TREVOR** *stops. The joint is burning his fingers.*)

TREVOR. Ow. Shit.

> (*He laughs. It's funny when things get burned.*)

> Wanna hit this?

JOANNE. ....Okay.

> (*He hands her the joint.*)

> What do you think of me? I mean, do you think of me?

TREVOR. Hell yeah I do.

JOANNE. No, If we were in the park and some guy came up and grabbed my purse and started running away would you chase him?

TREVOR. No.

> (*Pause.*)

JOANNE. Oh, okay.

TREVOR. Dude might have a *gun*.

JOANNE. (*denied*) Oh.

TREVOR. Do you wanna go to Pita Pit?

JOANNE. We just ate.

TREVOR. Nah, I'll just go on my way home.

(*Ow.*)

JOANNE. .....You're not staying over?

TREVOR. Nah, I wanna get an early start tomorrow.

(*He reaches for his backpack and starts to rustle through it.*)

JOANNE. Why haven't we – why haven't you wanted to – in like four days?

TREVOR. Whoa, huh?

JOANNE. We haven't had sex in four days.

TREVOR. Whoa – uh. Right. I was gonna tell you. God doesn't want me to be having sex right now. He told me. He wants me to think about other stuff.

(*Oddly, this touches* **JOANNE**.)

JOANNE. Oh – Right – okay. Of course. I'm sorry. So I guess I'll just see you Sunday.

TREVOR. What's going on Sunday?

JOANNE. My birthday.

TREVOR. Oh, yeah. Yeah, hmm.

JOANNE. What?

TREVOR. Hmm, I don't know. I got a lot of reading to do for that class.

JOANNE. Oh.

TREVOR. Lots of reading and that's when I was going to do it. Keirkegaard.

JOANNE. Okay.

TREVOR. No, I mean, I'll try, but I don't know.

JOANNE. No, it's no big deal, we could, um, some other time. But you said. We were going to walk to the water and look at it. We were going to get stoned and eat cake.

TREVOR. Yeah, sorry, Joanne, I care about you, Sorry I did that. But I have a lot of work to do.

JOANNE. Reading? Stuff to read?

TREVOR. Yeah. If I'm ever gonna, like, GET there, if I'm ever gonna be this rad mad rich famous philosopher dude who saves all humanity from destroying themself then I have to read, everything. Like, Russian stuff and Emily Dickinson and the newspaper.

JOANNE. I know. I don't want to distract you or anything. I just. It's my birthday. And as you get older, birthdays are less of thing involving cake and roller skates and more of a sad, sad problem that puts you early to bed.

(*Pause. He looks at her. He doesn't get it. He gets up, moves away from her, gets read to leave. She watches, desperately.*)

I was gonna kill myself. Right before we met.

TREVOR. No *way*. Like how?

JOANNE. I was in the beginning stages of planning.

TREVOR. Were you going shoot yourself?

JOANNE. Probably something – more – something less – um – something prettier. I'd swallow some nail polish remover?

TREVOR. Would that work?

JOANNE. I don't know.

TREVOR. *(suddenly serious)* Killing yourself is selfish cause God doesn't like people messing with his things. He wants to be the one who decides when you die, he doesn't want you to do it.

JOANNE. Yeah – well – I didn't do it, so.

TREVOR. You shouldn't.

JOANNE. Would you miss me?

TREVOR. Uh -

JOANNE. No, I'm not going to, that's what I'm saying, now that you're – you saved me. I don't know what I'd – Thank you. I'm sorry. I'm stoned. I think I'm saying thank you.

(*She touches him. Yes, please.*)

TREVOR. *(smiling)* Dang, birthday girl. You look hot.

(*He begins to kiss her neck. He goes for it. Gradually, she gives in, clinging to him, desperately.*)

V.

(**DIANE** *and* **TREVOR**. *at the water, a pier, leaning over the railing. They drink 40's, Heineken.* **TREVOR** *has a few empty ones next to him.*

Oh, And Sometimes during this scene, We can see **JOANNE**, *somewhere else, calling and calling him. Sometimes he notices, sometimes he doesn't.*

TREVOR. Whoa – it's freakin creepy out here – like a story.

(**TREVOR**'*s attention has turned back to his 40. Pause.*)

DIANE. It's not so bad. I get patrol out here sometimes. Pretty peaceful. No, every now and then, there's some weirdo trying to light his shoe on fire or some couple screaming at each other cause somebody's cheating or somebody's a baby daddy, but it's usually pretty calm.

TREVOR. Man, if anybody tried to fuck with you, if anybody tried to mess with you or steal your shit, I'd fucking, I'd beat their ass *down*.

(*He mimes this 'beating their ass down.'*)

They'd be sorry.

DIANE. Listen – I don't want you to think that I'm out here – with you – to initiate anything, I just, I've been meaning to brush up on my Philosophy. I thought it might be interesting. That's why I called. I want to make it perfectly clear that I am *way* too old for you.

(*He chugs, a whole lot. Burps, but endearing.*)

TREVOR. Whoa, you're a cop, hell yeah. Diane. That must be rad.

DIANE. Yeah, it's –

TREVOR. Telling people what to do all the time. I say *fuck the po-lice!* Nah, I'm kidding. You like being a cop, is it pretty rad, some power trip?

DIANE. No, It's not like that. I like helping people. My Dad used to do it, too.

TREVOR. Oh fuck, did he die?

DIANE. No. He got kicked out for playing too many practical jokes. Being too silly. He has a sick sense of humor. He got all the sense of humor so I got stuck with none.

(**TREVOR** *just nods, faux-understanding.*)

That was a joke.

TREVOR. (*not getting it.*) Oh. Cool.

Nah, but *helping.* Hell yeah.

I'm gonna help, too. I'm gonna solve the problems of the *universe.* And today I just figured out how. I was ridin my board through the park and God told me how.

DIANE. Oh yeah? How?

TREVOR. I'm gonna get rid of money.

DIANE. That's pretty ambitious.

TREVOR. (*Dead serious*) Don't tell anyone, though.

DIANE. (*unable to read him*) …I won't….?

TREVOR. Diane. Wow. You have a great face. Very real.

DIANE. Um. How old are you?

TREVOR. Uh. Let's see. (*Pause.*) 25. I brought us a stoog.

DIANE. What?

(*Again, with the impish smile, he produces a joint, raising his eyebrows*)

Oh, you've gotta be kidding me. I'm too old for that.
TREVOR. You're not old, you're beautiful.
DIANE. Oh, they can't go together?
TREVOR. Just my Mom. My Mom's old and beautiful, but that's it.

(**TREVOR** *lights the joint. Takes a few drags. Holds it out to her.*)

DIANE. You realize you're trying to get a cop stoned, don't you?
TREVOR. You said you used to write on walls.
DIANE. You remember.
TREVOR. Hell yeah.
DIANE. Yeah, I used to smoke.
TREVOR. Well then think of it as remembering.

(*She smiles. A pause. She smokes with him. Few beats.* **TREVOR** *hits the joint, repeatedly, and we see how badly he needs it.*)

DIANE. When I was a kid the cool kids used to dress like surfers. We didn't live anywhere near water.

I was kinda one of them. It was where all the guys – were. All the good ones, and all the girls knew it. You want a guy like that? You gotta learn the ways of the water person.

I think. Yeah.

But when I say I was ONE of them – I mean – I – shadowed them, like some kind of patient puppy.

And we would, um. We would write our names on things. Leave marks. Draw a tree, a joint. A river, some guy's name, draw over it and over and over. Magic markers, number two pencils that we kept in our teeth and behind our ears, ammo, instruments. We did it – So – so that – when we saw it – we'd know that we had been there. *I was here.* Yesterday wasn't a bad dream, or a good dream, it was real, because there's the proof. I swear, when we left that school, we – we left it full of names.

(*Pause.*)

But I didn't fuck any of them, no sir. Not then. I had priorities then. I believed in love.

(*She stops. She lets herself really realize this. She looks at* **TREVOR**, *embarrassed.*)

TREVOR. Yeah, dude. Love.

DIANE. Yeah. Love.

(**TREVOR** *burns his lips with the last of the joint, tosses it into the water.*)

TREVOR. Cashed. (*He turns and looks at her.*) I could be a cop if I wanted.

(**DIANE** *smiles.*)

DIANE. What'd you come here for really? You wanted? You on the run?

(**TREVOR** *is suddenly serious.*)

TREVOR. No, uh, nah. I worked for my Mom, after college, hung out. And uh there was this girl there. I was thinking of marrying. But then I was like nah, fuck that, I need to like journey first. I need to like, solve the post-structuralist problems of the universe.

DIANE. So you don't wanna get married?

TREVOR. Not yet. Gotta findthe right lady, first, or make sure I got the right one.

(*He smiles at her. She blushes hard.*)

DIANE. Nah – I don't want to get married. I don't think ever. Definitely not. (*Pause.*)

I don't usually do this.

TREVOR. What?

DIANE. Have okay conversations with guys when I'm not shit-faced.

TREVOR. You want another beer?

DIANE. No thanks. I don't, NEED to be drunk, I just feel better. You know. An excuse to be loose.

(**TREVOR** *starts doing air guitar through this, first a little, then big.*)

TREVOR. An excuse to be *loose*.

That should go in a song. Yeah, I write songs sometimes. I play the guitar.

I'm pretty good.

DIANE. (*liking this*) Yeah?

TREVOR. No, I suck. I'm gonna write one for you though. And it's gonna be called – DIANE – WITH THE EYES – LIKE THE OCEAN.

(*He begins to perform said song, like it is the bestest most important song ever.*)

And it's gonna go – Diane, your eyes are like the ocean, blue like my soul, and when I think about your pretty face, it makes me wanna ROCK AND ROLL

(*It turns into a bit of a punk ballad, he rocks out a bit, but it's a bit cute.* **DIANE** *laughs. He hangs himself over the railing, far.*)

Let's fucking JUMP in this WATER.

DIANE. Uh, *no.*

TREVOR. No, come on, we'll be like freakin FISH, it'll be rad. We'll ride the waves.

DIANE. There aren't any waves, it's a river.

TREVOR. No, like, the little ones that the water taxi's make and shit, hell yeah, we'll ride those like freakin five footers, lady, let's do it. Let's get in.

(*He takes his shirt off. It's nice. She blushes.*)

DIANE. I like it right here, thanks.

TREVOR. Come on!

(*He jumps up on the rail.*)

DIANE. Oh my God, get *down*. You're going to fall in.

TREVOR. (*teasing*) Am I scaring you, Am I scaring you?

DIANE. YES!

TREVOR. (*shouting, out*) I'M SCARING DIANE!

DIANE. If you fall in, you can't get out. I'm not getting you out. And it is very, VERY illegal.

TREVOR. (*fake falling*) WHOA!

DIANE. (*reaching for him*) FUCK!

(*He laughs.* **TREVOR** *begins to yell for no reason, like a little boy.*)

TREVOR. DIANE THE BEAUTIFUL COP LADY DOESN'T WANT TO BE A FISH WITH ME!

DIANE. Get the fuck down or I'm leaving.

TREVOR. DIANE AND I ARE GOING TO SOLVE THE SOCIALOGICAL MARXIST CAPITALIST PHENOMENOLOGICAL MARXIST PROBLEMS OF THE

UNIVERSE ONE FISH AT A TIME!

DIANE. You're going to get us in trouble.

TREVOR. FREE TIBET! MAKE – MARIJUANA LEGAL! PIZZA FOR EVERYONE! JESUS LOVES YOU! PUNK ROCK! GREEN PEACE! ME AND **DIANE** ARE DRUNK AND HER DAD USED TO BE A COP!

(*He laughs at what he feels might have been a joke.* **DIANE** *starts to gather her things.*)

DIANE. I'm out. This is ridiculous. You're like a little kid. I'm out.

TREVOR. Oh, come on, I'm just messing.

DIANE. No. I'm going. I'm too old for this.

(*He jumps down, right in front of her.*)

TREVOR. To old for a kiss?

DIANE. What?

TREVOR. I wanna make love to you.

DIANE. (*but frozen*) I'm going.

TREVOR. You've got something on your face:

DIANE. What?

TREVOR. Me.

(*He moves in fast, before she can protest, and kisses her. She leans against him like a dead fish, at first, flopping, then falls into the kiss, which is really good. She pulls away, stunned. Pause. She falls in love. From somewhere, a red flower falls. They both stare at it.*)

DIANA. Huh.

TREVOR. Huh.

(*He picks it up.*)

Dare me to eat it? I'll eat it.

DIANA. No – Don't!

> (**TREVOR** *puts it in her hair. It falls.* **DIANA** *puts it right back. She kisses him. Lights down on this.*)

> (*Only* **JOANNE** *remains. She leaves a frantic, sad voicemail. During, she tries very hard to be neither frantic or sad. Her party hat sags.*)

JOANNE. Hey – hey you. I just wanted to say – um – I'm sorry you're dead. I'm sorry you died. Because you must be dead.

You must be stuck under a building, under a piece of a parking lot. You must have been hit by a car on your board. You must be in the hospital. I hope it doesn't hurt too much. I hope it doesn't sting. (*Pause.*)

I guess I just – well – sorry, again, that you are dead. But call me. Call me anyways, so that I know that you are? Or aren't? Just so I know? (*Pause.*) Oh yeah, and happy birthday.

Oh wait, it's not your birthday. It's mine.

(*She hangs up.*)

VI.

(The club, again. Mike drops. **GEORGIA.***)*

GEORGIA. Sleeping Around.
And it also happens that
I am tired of fucking,
I am over it.
I am tired of having to suck
before I know what the fuck
he wants most when he's hungry;
what the hell he likes to wear
or does he even care about
that sort of thing,
or would he rather hide inside
old sweatshirts that remind him of his high school.
And it happens I'm tired of
doing it with my eyes closed.
It just so happens I'm sick of meaningless dick
attached to a body that lies in my bed that
might as well be dead
with how much it doesn't care
to touch me.
I'm tired of his having to meet his friend in the a.m.
when I want to stay in
and wrap myself around this body
that I bonded with.
I want to talk until
and I know exactly what he was like
when he was eight and whether or not he likes cake
and what movie he last saw
and why he fucking hated it or
would see it again, twice,

with me,
because I'm a thing with a face
and a name that goes with it
that he might think about taking with him
when he leaves my apartment.

It just so happens that I am tired of repeating myself.
I am tired of writing about this
when all I want is a kiss that
lasts seven years and fills my room with flowers.

It happens, right now,
that I am a copy cat.
I am emulating a poem I once read about wanting to
 be dead
written by A Chilean man who
I'd probably fuck if I had any luck
which I probably would
cause I'm good and a girl and easily pushed
to fucking with no specifics,
none at all,
just reduced to an act like algebra.

(*Scattered applause.* **GEORGIA** *is livid and sad by the end of this. She peers out into the crowd, looking. Where is he? And then she's gone.*)

(**JOANNE** *appears, sitting in a chair, legs spread wide. She inspects herself. She picks up a gun. She inspects herself.*)

(*And then* **ANNA** *appears in her backyard, as before. She hums and strums the harp. All of the sudden, beautiful purple flowers softly begin to fall, and white ones the kinds that float in dishes, just a few. She notices. She smiles. She laughs and begins to gather them in her hands. She dances around inside of them.*)

END ACT I

ACT II

I.

(*The backyard.* **ANNA** *is lying on the ground, making a list with a crayon. Her happy ass is in the air. Next to her, a pink purse.*)

(*The sounds of birds and flowers.*)

ANNA. Tampons? Check.

Pamprin? Check.

An overwhelming sense of joy – check.

Mascara – check. Boyfriend? Ew. Maxi pads? Ew.

Pubic hair, kind of.

Strawberry Starbursts and a whole bag of just red skittles – check.

Back up pair of underwear the pair with the purple lace at the top that I bought with my babysitting money when Mom was trying to the get the night manager to notice her new Bra. Check.

List of important items – check.

Pretty? Yes. Plans – not yet.

(*She folds the list and places it into her purse. She pulls the purse onto her lap. She sits and waits. She looks at her harp. She slides a foot towards it. It falls over.*)

Oops.

II.

(The park, by the playground. **GEORGIA** *and* **TREVOR**. *sit on a bench.* **TREVOR** *eats a giant sandwich. Somewhere else,* **JOANNE** *is calling and calling and calling him. He checks his phone. He turns it off. He eats more sandwich.* **GEORGIA** *watches kids play. We can hear their cute kid sounds, and the sound of a sandwich.)*

GEORGIA. Ohhhhh look at that one. The fat one in that blue Eskimo suit thing? So cute. I could eat him. What a fat little marshmallow baby. I want that one.

*(***TREVOR** *doesn't respond. The sandwich is better than any conversation, ever.)*

So uh – how you been?

TREVOR. Excellent.

GEORGIA. I'm performing tonight.

TREVOR. Rad.

GEORGIA. Yeah, I thought you might, wanna check it out.

TREVOR. Tonight, hmmm. Yeah, I don't know. I should probably stay in and do some work.

GEORGIA. *(dry)* Yeah, how's it going?

TREVOR. Fucking sick.

GEORGIA. Good.

I wrote a new poem. It's about you.

TREVOR. Whoa, really?

GEORGIA. It's good. No, I don't know, it's bad. If I say it's good then it's bad.

(Pause. **TREVOR** *eats.)*

Hey Remember the first time we – at that stupid dirt

bar – when we –

TREVOR. When was that?

GEORGIA. Two months ago. The day I made up my new name. When I signed up for the poetry thing, where we met. I go to write my name down, but I didn't write my name, GEORGIA, I mean, fuck all names that are also secretly states or flowers or feelings.

(*Pause. Trevor eats.*)

You know what I wrote? AJ HAWTHORNE. Because then I could be man or woman and from anywhere, just about. It wouldn't automatically be, here's this girl just moved here from Georgia to flee her unbelievably unoriginal parents who are more than happy to work for Food Lion. You know what that's like? When the Family sized frozen lasagnas go on sale it's a goddamn EVENT. So AJ Hawthorne, that's what I wrote, and I go onstage, and I'm maybe going to shit myself, and then I speak.

TREVOR. Yeah, was it a Thursday?

GEORGIA. I don't know. Point being, it was about love. What I was saying, the poem. It was about, yeah.

Because what else is there to *truthfully* write about when you're 22 and pretty stupid and come from a stable family environment? So I was talking about love, about how it's like apples or vacuum cleaners or something stretched.

And I'm doing the thing, and I'm scared, and no one's listening, and I feel like a ghost. I'm trying not to care that people are more interested in getting shit-faced than hearing something true. A tear kind of came and was like hanging there threatening to fall and blow my cover. I didn't wanna cry, I didn't wanna be that girl crying all bad and wet.

And I looked out, and I saw you, sitting there in the back. You know what you were doing?

TREVOR. What?

GEORGIA. You were nodding, And smiling, You were shooting me this affirmation across the place.

TREVOR. You looked hot, in the lights, all up there. You looked famous. You're freakin sick, G, you're good. You've got real talent. I can write poems, too. Yeah, I'm gonna write a poem.

GEORGIA. You don't really think that.

TREVOR. No, I'm definitely going to write a poem. I can do that, too.

GEORGIA. No, you don't really think that I'm – hot, good.

TREVOR. Yeah I do.

GEORGIA. No. because if you really thought that, you'd wanna hang out with me. Be with me.

TREVOR. I'm with you right now.

GEORGIA. (*desperately*) No, what I'm TRYING to say is – no matter what I do, I – I can't seem to find – and I thought that *you* – maybe still, maybe you – are you *it?* I mean, are you him? If not you than who?

(**ANNA** *walks by, bouncing a bouncy ball, dragging her harp, happy, looking younger.* **TREVOR** *stares.*)

TREVOR. Say what?

(**ANNA** *is gone.*)

GEORGIA. I was just wondering if – whether or not you –

TREVOR. Listen – sorry, like, I haven't called a lot lately. I

just, man. Been busy.
GEORGIA. …No, I haven't been calling *you.*
TREVOR. Oh yeah?
GEORGIA. Yeah, you didn't notice?
TREVOR. Nah, I –
GEORGIA. Nevermind.
> (*Pause.* **GEORGIA** *looks out again at the playing children. This calms her. She smiles.*)

My favorite is when babies have adult faces. You can look at them and see exactly what they're going to look like when they grow up. Baby adult faces with credit cards and student loans, already. Like they don't even know peace.

(*Pause.*)

I was an ugly baby. I looked like a turd. I bet you were fucking cute. But you had to grow into that nose. I had to grow into mine. Took up my whole freaking face. The Texas of my face. Yours, yours is a bit more, Oklahoma. (*Pause.*) Did You ever want one?

TREVOR. What?
GEORGIA. A kid.
TREVOR. I have one.
GEORGIA. What? Fuck off.
TREVOR. No, sorta.
GEORGIA. You sort of have a kid?
TREVOR. When I was fifteen, okay? I kinda got my girlfriend pregnant and she had it we gave it up for adoption. I guess that's what you get for doin' it in the ocean.
GEORGIA. ….I haven't heard this.

TREVOR. Well, fuck yeah, it's in the past.

GEORGIA. So you have a ten year old child.

TREVOR. (*engaged in sandwich*) Yeah. Hmm. Yeah, ten, I guess.

GEORGIA. Wow. Boy or girl?

TREVOR. Huh?

GEORGIA. Was it a boy or a girl?

TREVOR. Oh, a dude.

GEORGIA. Don't you ever, I mean, don't you ever – wonder – what – what if he tries to find you? When he's twenty one and pissed off? / What if he tracks you down?

TREVOR. Nah. Yeah. Damn. This is the best gyro ever.

(*Pause as he eats.*)

GEORGIA. So you have a kid.

TREVOR. Yeah.

GEORGIA. A child.

TREVOR. Yeah, one of those.

GEORGIA. …..Okay.

(*She falls silent.*)

TREVOR. Whoa, uh, are you pissed? Are you sad or something?

GEORGIA. Nah, don't –

(**TREVOR** *doesn't know what to say.*)

TREVOR. I, uh, I told you, I told you when we first hung out, we can have fun and all, but I'm here for one thing, God sent me and stuff.

GEORGIA. How. How did God send you? Did he buy your plane ticket?

TREVOR. He believes in me. He talks to me when I'm sleeping. He sends me messages.

GEORGIA. Just you?

TREVOR. Through like words and things I see and stuff. Clouds. Look at that cloud.

(*He points. He studies it.*)

Nah, nevermind.

I don't know. (*Pause.*)

All I know is I'm going to become the / raddest philosopher ever.

GEORGIA. The raddest philosopher ever. How's this for philosophy? I got pregnant.

(*Pause.*)

TREVOR. Oh. Man.

GEORGIA. Yeah.

TREVOR. That *sucks*. Who?

GEORGIA. Uh, *you*.

TREVOR. Man.

(*Pause.*)

Uh – dude. Man. Are we supposed to uh – am I supposed to uh – are we supposed to – cause I don't / believe in –

GEORGIA. You're supposed to say sorry.

TREVOR. Sorry.

GEORGIA. And then you're supposed to give me a kiss like the first kiss you gave me.

(*Pause.* **TREVOR** *looks around. He kisses her.* **JOANNE** *walks by. She sees this. She almost says something, but* *can't decide which inappropriate thing to say. Devastated, she hurries off.*)

PS. That's not how it was. It was like this.

(*She kisses him softly.*)

TREVOR. Oh.

GEORGIA. And then you're supposed to hold my hand.

TREVOR. Nah – um – sorry – I don't hold hands. It makes other people feel sad to get jealous. People who don't have anybody to hold hands with.

GEORGIA. Uh – oh. Awesome.

(*Pause.*)

Well It went away.

TREVOR. Huh? It?

GEORGIA. It fucking, fucking sucked.

TREVOR. Hmm. What?

GEORGIA. The baby, Trevor, FUCK. That thing that we made on accident. It went AWAY.

TREVOR. Wait, it –

GEORGIA. I guess I shoulda called you.

TREVOR. Damn.

GEORGIA. I'm sorry, awkward, I know, not the best, I mean, but at least I waited til you finished your lunch.

TREVOR. Yeah.

(*Long pause*)

GEORGIA. ....Can I have a fucking hug?

TREVOR. ....Yeah. Cool.

(*He hugs her. She really falls into it. They let it go. They both look out, watching the kids. Both are visibly disturbed. A leaf falls. Just one.)*

Oh sweet! A leaf!

(He picks it up, inspects it like an artifact.)

Oh man, leafs are so – look. Look. This leaf is alive.
GEORGIA. No, it's dead. That's why it fell.
TREVOR. Really? Oh.

(Pause. He thinks. He smiles.)

Hey. I got this for you.

(He offers the leaf to her.)

GEORGIA. No you didn't.
TREVOR. Yeah, I *did*.

(Somehow, this touches her. She smiles 30% and takes it. She begins to tear it apart, but softly.)

GEORGIA. We woulda had a cute kid.
TREVOR. I'm – not – I mean, I don't want –
GEORGIA. Oh. Trust me. I know.
TREVOR. Cool.
GEORGIA. I'd be a really good Mom.
TREVOR. Yeah you would.
GEORGIA. Yeah. Sometimes I just want one.

(Pause. They sit. She sneaks small looks at him and at his form.)

III.

(The brick wall, again. In the shadows, Night. **DIANE** *is on duty, in uniform. She and* **TREVOR** *are passing a joint between them, discreetly.* **TREVOR** *looks about nervously every time he hits it. Laughing, love. He kisses her, intermittently. Every now and then, he finds a piece of red flower in her hair and eats it. She likes this.)*

DIANE. No they *don't.*

TREVOR. Yes they *do.* Raccoons have two dicks, yeah they do.

DIANE. How do you know, you know any raccoons? What, you fuck a raccoon?

TREVOR. Dude, I'm not gay!

DIANE. Ha! You're not gay. I know you're not gay. In case you remember, I'm sleeping with you, We have sex. We've had sex eight and a half times.

TREVOR. Hey – dude – if I had a baby – if you had my baby –

DIANE. We're having a baby?

TREVOR. You wouldn't kill it would you or anything or let it go away?

DIANE. N – NEVER Never, Trevor. *(She laughs.)* Trevor. Trevor. That's your name.

TREVOR. That's my name.

(Yelling)

MY NAME IS TREVOR!

DIANE. *(but laughing)* Sshhh. Shhhhh. I'm on the job. I'm on the rag. Ha. I'm working.

TREVOR. Working how? Working is like STUPID. Working is for WHORES.

DIANE. W – *what?*

(*She laughs.*)

No – sshhhh – no – we're serious now. We're being serious.

I'm standing *guard*. I'm *guarding*. I'm supposed to watch out for a suspicious suspicion. There's a threat on that building, that's the back entrance across the street.

TREVOR. (*looking up*) That building is, like, *tall.*

(**TREVOR**'s *phone rings. He looks at it, ignores call.*)

DIANE. Taller than tall, tall.

TREVOR. If I wanted to blow something up, I would just do it. Nobody would stop me. I'd strap myself, I'd be strapped. If God asked me to do that, I'd do it.

(**DIANE** *turns tender.*)

DIANE. I love you.

TREVOR. What?

DIANE. Made you look.

TREVOR. Dude, they're kicking me out of housing.

DIANE. Wh – what?

TREVOR. Yeah somebody smelled my doob.

(*They crack up.*)

DIANE. Hey – you could – maybe you / could –

TREVOR. I want some birthday cake, is it somebody's birthday?

DIANE. Yeah – shitty Food Lion cake with Dinosaur frosting monsters – Oh my God. Grape soda.

TREVOR. All the time. Fucking *fritos*.

DIANE. You read my mind, how do you do that, you read my mind.

TREVOR. Yeah, you're pretty cool. Let me touch you.

DIANE. Okay.

(**TREVOR** *touches her.*)

Is there nobody else in the world but me? Am I the only one?

TREVOR. For sure.

(**JOANNE** *appears, sitting her apartment, in a chair, legs spread wide. She's leaving a voicemail.*)

JOANNE. I love with my whole self. That's bad.

DIANE. Can we hang out – all the time?

JOANNE. George says or he used to say I love with too much of myself and this scares boys I mean men it scares guys away.

DIANE. Like forever?

JOANNE. They feel like every piece of me: My elbows. And the things stuck in my small intestine. And my cuticles and my hair and my butt and my knees and all of my chins, they're all loving them at the same time.

DIANE. Cause you make me really happy.

JOANNE. It makes them feel small. To be loved that much. That's what George says. I guess this is why. Is that why? Did you have a nice birthday? I did not.

DIANE. Really, really happy. Like I don't even care. I don't even care.

JOANNE. That black girl was pretty. Her lip liner was uneven.

I bet you didn't even notice. I bet she's got a beautiful spot like a perfect chocolate cupcake, that makes a sound like 'ding'. better than mine. I bet you ate it.

DIANE. What do you think about me?

JOANNE. Guess what? Goodbye.

(She turns away. She spreads her legs further. Very apart. She brings the gun slowly between her legs. Lights out on her.)

TREVOR. You're a sweet lady. You got a big heart, I can tell. You get stoned with me.

DIANE. Yeah, I haven't, I haven't, I mean, why isn't this *legal?*

TREVOR. Exactly, exactly! Diana!

DIANE. Diane.

TREVOR. We're gonna, we're gonna start a war against the government! A government that prohibits its citizens from fulfilling their basic need of getting *fucked* up. It's not right. It's a need, man. It's shouldn't be a luxury, it's something that's gotta happen.

DIANE. What're you gonna do?

TREVOR. About what?

DIANE. About anything, tell me your plans, tell me all your plans. I wanna know everything inside your head. Lay it all out, lay it on me. I wanna have your kid and buy it a little swimming pool,1 ft. deep, and fill it with lemonade and I want to watch you while you teach it to swim. What are you plans? What's in your head? Say everything please.

TREVOR. Oh. Hmm. I dunno. I was gonna do something, today. *(Pause.)* Yeah, I was gonna do something important. What was it? I got stoned – Went to the park. Was gonna find somewhere else to live – like I was gonna find some old lady with some apartment above her bake store and she was gonna say *hey, you can live up there for free* and then I Met up with you – Pretty Lady.

(*grinning*)

Pretty Lady.

(*He kisses her, deep.*)

Come on, let's go. I wanna take you somewhere and take your clothes off, one by one.

DIANE. I gotta stay here, I'm at work.

TREVOR. Doing what?

DIANE. I'm supposed to look out. I'm keeping watch. It's my job. Some of us have jobs.

TREVOR. Hey I gotta job. I'm a cool mother fucker *and* a soldier of the Lord.

DIANE. I'm getting paid to look *out* for creepy mother fuckers, dudes with games up their sleeves. Guys that look like they have nowhere to go, like they got games in their eyes.

Like that guy over there.

TREVOR. Where?

DIANE. That guy over there with the, what the fuck, is he?

TREVOR. (*freaking out, a bit*) What, is he watching us? Is he watching us? Is that dude a cop?

DIANE. No, that guy. That guy. Oh fuck. Oh no. Ohnoohnoohno.

(*She reaches for her radio.*)

This is officer Wright reporting, 66th and Right, unit five. All units, suspicious. Suspicious, uh. Uh.
TREVOR. Activity, activity!
DIANE. SUSPICIOUS ACTIVITY!

(Diane Reaches for her gun. As she does so, lights out, fast. Sirens, explosion, big. Black.)

IV.

(*The club, mike drops.* **GEORGIA**.)

GEORGIA. And what is it like to be dead?
>Is it like a bad kiss
>or is this more like it:
>It's gotta be something like when I
>go home to my folks.
>Do we communicate?
>Nope.
>But my Dad has a telescope
>which he set up out back
>to relax and gaze at stars that
>really are bigger than our big house.
>He looks through the thing at things burning
>big and beyond him and he will google the things
>to try and understand them.
>But my world is small.
>I can't seem to dream beyond my
>new bootcut jeans that
>I will wear, religiously,
>as I meander towards dying which
>could be tomorrow or in fifty years,
>slowly because of cigarettes.
>My friend called and said his Dad is dead,
>this morning.
>I think I'll include this here.
>His dead Dad is dead
>and I'm thinking of the head
>my little brother is probably getting from short girls
>being that he is now a big man,

meandering slowly towards dying.
But my friend's dead Dad is dead.
He found him on the carpet
with a dead dying heart.
I wonder how his mother is
and which black dress she'll wear on Wednesday.

My live Dad is living to look at stars
through an expensive thing
that will teach him more about being small,
comparatively.
I am glad my live Dad is living,
but why?
Maybe it's in the sky.
Maybe we can look at it together.

(*She bows. Few claps.* **GEORGIA** *starts to go, but then comes back.*)

Does any one want to make love to me? I have four down pillows and a very soft duvet. Are you broken? Me too. I have an excellent memory and will memorize every word you say but not use it against you. I make a mean morning breakfast scramble, complete with toast and coffee however you like it. I give mediocre head, but I swallow. Does any one want to cuddle?

(*The lights start to go down on her. In The dark, she yells*)

Does anyone want to make love to me?

(*Pause.*)

If you're tired – I could make love to *you*. Instead.

(*She is gone.*)

V.

(**DIANE**, *at a table. Bandages on her hands, burns, but she is happy. Her* **MOTHER** *makes coffee. Same* **MOM** *as earlier but older, rustier.*)

MOTHER. You were *stoned?*

DIANE. It's a long story.

MOTHER. Are you a drug addict? Thirty Four years old, you decide to start using drugs?

DIANE. Mom, I'm fine.

MOTHER. You got fired.

DIANE. I know. Thank you. I forgot.

MOTHER. You don't have a job.

DIANE. But I didn't die. Aren't you happy? I could've.

MOTHER. You weren't that close to it, I saw it on the news. Nobody died. It was a pretty sad attempt at an explosion if you ask me. Just a few broken windows and dead old washing machines. That's all. Don't be so dramatic.

DIANE. I still *could've.* Do you care? Be sad for a second, can't you kiss me all over my face and say *my baby*?

MOTHER. Is that what you want?

DIANE. I was SCARED.

(**MOM** *sighs, goes to* **DIANE**, *and sans passion, kisses her in a stiff triangle: cheek forehead, cheek.*)

MOTHER. My baby. My baby. My baby.

Your father is going to kill you.

DIANE. Dad got fired from the force for putting mace in the all the air conditioner units. Dad will have to deal with it.

MOTHER. What are you going to do now?

DIANE. Well – I – Mom – I – I think I'm – getting married!

MOTHER. To who?

DIANE. The guy, I told you about the guy!

MOTHER. What guy?

DIANE. I told you about him. He's a *philosopher.*

MOTHER. They still have those? What for? What *guy?*

DIANE. The guy. I've been seeing. I think I, I think he's it.

MOTHER. It.

DIANE. It.

MOTHER. And why?

DIANE. How he makes me feel. How he looks at me. Like I'm the only person in the world.

MOTHER. Oh, that's the first time anybody's ever said *that.*

DIANE. You know I wouldn't say it if I didn't mean it.

(MOTHER *pours the coffee.*)

MOTHER. This isn't study hall. Your biological clock is ticking. If you don't conceive, holy shit, if you don't conceive within the next *year* Diane, your children will have a thirty percent chance of having downs syndrome. I always pity those grandmothers pushing around those little almond eyed kids. You know they love them but who else ever will?

Is he nice? Is he tall? Does he pay? Does he tell you're pretty? Because you are. (*Pause.*) You always had the nicest hands.

(DIANE *looks at her paws.*)

MOTHER. What's his family like?

DIANE. I don't know.

MOTHER. I'll meet him.

DIANE. Don't embarrass me.

MOTHER. Never.

DIANE. Be happy for me. Are you happy for me?

MOTHER. Yes.

(Pause. She puts coffee down in front of both of them, sits.)

Because I don't want to – but I have to bring up Robert / and how

DIANE. WE DON'T SAY THAT NAME. I don't know that name. That name is a dead word.

MOTHER. It took a long time to cancel all the catering and flowers. There are still envelopes in the attic. I'm just asking, are you SURE?

DIANE. YES. WE HAVE SEX.

(Pause.)

MOTHER. Alright. *(Pause.)* I understand.

DIANE. You do?

MOTHER. No, I do, I get it.

I used to want to make love to a musician. So that I could go watch him make his music, in some remotely crowded place, and I could sit in a corner and watch him and think, I make love to that person. That body is mine.

That's all I ever wanted. But none of them ever wanted me. They like girls who can use their hair as blankets and women who were raped as children.

Why is it whenever you want one thing you end up

with the exact opposite? What sort of fate is that?

Well I pushed this aside. I pushed it way deep down in, forgot it. But it was about ten years ago when I saw a dirty man on the street with a guitar and I looked at him and I loved him and I stood and watched.

I gave him fifty dollars for his guitar. He only asked for twenty. He was hungry and he had a kitten on a string that needed to eat.

I took the guitar home to your father, I said here. I said, learn to play this, or I might accidentally no longer love you. He took it in his hands. It was foreign, but I said, pretend it's a gun.

DIANE. Did he learn to play?

MOTHER. One chord before giving up. But it was the best five minutes of my life.

DIANE. Why?

MOTHER. Because just for a moment, what I had and what I wanted were the same thing.

(**DIANE** *nods. She holds her coffee between hurt paws.*)

(*Lights shift to the backyard, Nighttime.* **ANNA** *sits with her purse, still waiting, bored.* **MOM** *enters, weary.*)

MOM. (*O.S.*) ANNA- Anna, I'm home –

(**MOM** *enters, weary. Her date outfit wilts.*) ....What are you doing?

ANNA. Waiting.
MOM. For what?
ANNA. Life.

(**MOM**'s *eyes land on the harp.*)

MOM. What happened to your harp?

ANNA. It died. What happened to your date?

(**MOM** *is quiet for a moment.*)

MOM. My date decided that, um – halfway through the appetizer, we decided that, well he, he decided that –

(*She looks at* **ANNA.** *Ow.*)

Let's just say I should've borrowed your face.

ANNA. That sucks.

MOM. Did you finish that letter to your cousin?

ANNA. *Mom.*

MOM. He's nice enough to write you letters, you should write him back. What do they say, anyways? (*Pause.*) Anna, what do they say?

ANNA. Nothing, all kinds of stuff.

MOM. Well, write him back.

ANNA. *Fine.*

(*Anna pulls cute notebook and pen out of purse.* **MOM** *begins to wander towards the house.*)

Where're you going?

MOM. Nowhere.

ANNA. To do what?

MOM. Nothing.

(**MOM** *is gone* **ANNA** *writes.*)

ANNA. Dear Cuz,

(*Lights fade here.* **ANNA**'s *letter fades into* **V.O.**, *music.*)

ANNA. V.O. Thanks for all your letters. They are cool. I thought I would write you one back. I am doing good.

My mom is sad a lot all the time but I have been going to the mall and the movies with my friends.

Yesterday at the mall I tried sushi and it was yuck. I did not like how it felt in my mouth, how can people eat that shiz? Also yesterday we were at the mall and Sara and I were in the bathroom behind the Chickfila by the payphones. And she got out a sharp needle and she said go get me some ice so I did and then I said *what for?*

And she said, *I want to pierce my ear.* I said *why, you've already got your ears pierced?* She said I *want to do it again, I want second and third holes, I want more,* and I said why, and she said *I don't like the way I look* So she closed her eyes and I pressed it through her ear and I could feel it pop through all of her skins and it bled all over my hand. And she cried but she said it was okay because it was a good hurt.

Well I guess thank you again for all your letters and I hope you are having fun doing what you are doing where you are doing it. Maybe when you come back sometime we can hang out. Love, Anna.

TREVOR *appears, walking down the street, reading the letter, smiling, big.*

TREVOR *crosses paths with* **MONA**, *who is struggling with a bunch of grocery bags. She smiles at him. He smiles, slow, back at her, like a big little boy. He keeps walking, engrossed in letter.*

MONA. I could really use some help, here.

(*Pause. He walks towards her. Lights.*)

V.

(**MONA'S** *apartment, but again with the brick. The kitchen. Lights* **MONA**, *47, enters. She is quite beautiful with gi-normous breasts; these beauties are hidden beneath sensible, modest clothing; she appears to be quite the cookie baker.* **TREVOR** *follows her in, carrying two huge shopping bags full of assorted grocery goods. It's nighttime.*)

TREVOR. Uh, Where'd you want these?

MONA. Counter's fine. You're such a dear for helping me. I really am such a dummy sometimes, buying more stuff than I can carry up my own stairs! I'm such a twat.

(*He schleps them on the counter, but neatly.*)

TREVOR. Well, you asked, and I can't say no to pretty ladies.

MONA. Aw. That's sweet. You are twelve years old. Have a seat.

TREVOR. No, it's alright, I gotta/ get

MONA. You gotta, you gotta take a seat right there and Mona's going to make you some hot cocoa.

TREVOR. Hmm.

MONA. Would You like that?

TREVOR. Hot cocoa is *epic*.

MONA. So sit.

(*He sits. Looks around.*)

(*She starts removing things, one at a time, from the bags, and places them neatly, methodically, one a time, in their proper place. 7 giant boxes of raisins. A bag of swirly straws. 4 cans of whipped cream. Cat food. Toothpicks. Artichokes. Splenda. Spam.*)

TREVOR. Are you having a party?

MONA. What for?

TREVOR. I don't know, you just look like you're getting ready for a party?

MONA. No sir!

TREVOR. You got a cat, huh.

MONA. (*puzzled*) No.

(**TREVOR** *looks around.*)

TREVOR. Where's your husband?

MONA. Prison.

TREVOR. What?

MONA. Prison.

TREVOR. What for?

MONA. Beating me up. And I have an MFA. You can't beat on somebody with an MFA.

TREVOR. Yeah, I want some of those one day, too.

MONA. (*Having finished putting everything away, she looks at him.*) So would you like to touch them?

TREVOR. What?

MONA. You've been looking at them since you got here.

TREVOR. At what?

MONA. (*She goes to him. Puts her boobs in his face.*) Go ahead. Go ahead or I'll scream.

(*He smiles. He loosens up. He puts his hands on them.*)

Just so you know, I'm 47 years old and much too old

for you.

TREVOR. Damn, no way! Were you in the Holocaust?

MONA. No, but I've been to the moon.

TREVOR. No way.

MONA. What's your name, sweetie?

TREVOR. Trevor.

MONA. Trevor, you are a fine young man.

TREVOR. Thank you. You have a nice voice. And your hair looks like cotton candy. That's cool.

MONA. Trevor, I'd like to tie you to the chair.

TREVOR. Why's that?

MONA. And give you a hummer.

TREVOR. A, ?

MONA. A blowjob. Is that alright?

TREVOR. (*relaxing*) Hell yeah.

MONA. Don't move.

(*She puts on the cocoa. She gets an extension cord. With it, she ties him to the chair. Tight. During.*)

MONA. Did I mention I've been to the moon? I've been seven times. I walked on it. It was like here but gushier and opposite.

TREVOR. They're just letting people up to the moon now? I wanna go!

MONA. I used to be an astronaut.

TREVOR. No *way*.

MONA. Yes. Then They fired me.

TREVOR. Why?

MONA. Because of my temper.

(*She's done tying him.*)

How's that?

TREVOR. Rad.

MONA. (*inspecting him*) Aren't you going to get turned on?

TREVOR. What's that?

MONA. You're not turned on.

TREVOR. Oh, uh, stage fright.

MONA. This isn't going to work if you're not turned on.

TREVOR. Tell me more about the moon.

MONA. It wasn't just the moon. It was all other planets, too.

TREVOR. You were on all the planets?

MONA. Yes. You know Neptune. It's made of raisins.

TREVOR. No way.

MONA. Uh huh.

See, Trevor, all the planets outside of earth are giant versions of things that are really small here.

I spent most of my younger years studying the stars and the air and the earth and planets. I slept in my clothes. I looked at the sky until my face fell off. I breathed in equations. And my husband, he, well, he is a very angry mathematician who I swear would hunt and kill and eat numbers if he could. He would have infinity for breakfast if I could pin it down for him and fry it.

He was always upset at the illogicalness of everything including my face and my hair and my butt and this made us very happy together, somehow. How much we wanted to solve things – but Love has no mass or density. It floats like feelings.

We became very angry because there *had* to be an answer to everything but we couldn't even answer the questions we had for each other. And this is how we fell in love.

This went on for a while. Then I went off into space. There, I could see intangible things in the air. Words become realized as physical things, and passed back and forth. This is, by the way, in the future, will be the way in which Robots will make Love to Each other.

And when I got back, he had forgotten that he was supposed to love me while I was away, and he showed me this with his fist and my grandmother's frying pan.

What's my Name?

TREVOR. Mona.

MONA. Are you turned on yet?

TREVOR. Uh, no. Sorry, I. Just gimmee a minute, damn.

MONA. I'm going to empty your pockets.

(She starts doing so. She pulls out a wallet, a joint, a lighter, some cash, a piece of blue chalk.)

You're an artist?

TREVOR. I'm a Philosopher. I'm on this rad, rad philosophical journey. I've got this plan to / solve the like crazy –

MONA. Does that get you hard?

TREVOR. What?

MONA. Talking about Philosophy?

TREVOR. I mean, No.

MONA. Then quit doing it.

(She pulls a chair, close to him.)

Want a genuine astronaut kiss?

TREVOR. Okay.

MONA. Hold your breathe.

Hold it.

(*He does so.*)

You're not really holding it.

(*She goes behind him. Covers his nose and mouth with her hands. For a bit. A while. It gets a bit scary.* **TREVOR** *starts to squirm. She's strong. He squirms, a lot. Is she trying to, ? Finally, she lets him go, fast, and kisses him fast, lets him go.*)

There, there are you dizzy?

TREVOR. (*gasping a bit*) What?

MONA. That's what it's like! That's what it's like to make love in Space! That's how the kisses feel!

(*She looks at him, again.*)

Oh, Trevor. You came. That's so cute.

TREVOR. Oh.

MONA. You liked that.

TREVOR. Untie me?

MONA. In a minute.

TREVOR. Maybe I should oughta –

MONA. You been with a lot of women, Trevor?

TREVOR. I don't know.

MONA. Yes, I bet ladies just love you. That body. I can tell through your stupid clothes. I'm going to get them off of you but honestly I'd rather drag it out. Somebody really put some time in to you. Your mother must be a real piece of work.

TREVOR. Yeah.

MONA. Is she?
TREVOR. I guess.
MONA. Is she a real piece of work?
TREVOR. She's dead.
MONA. Oh?
TREVOR. Dead.

(*Pause.*)

MONA. Diabetes?
TREVOR. No.
MONA. Airplane?
TREVOR. No.
MONA. Motocycle Mis-hap.
TREVOR. No.
MONA. Natural Disaster?
TREVOR. No.
MONA. Food poisoning?
TREVOR. No.
MONA. Falling.
TREVOR. No.
MONA. Drowning.
MONA. Sharks.
TREVOR. No.
MONA. Looking at you.
TREVOR. What?
MONA. Suicide.
TREVOR. Yes.

(*Pause.*)

MONA. Sleeping pills?

TREVOR. No.
MONA. Jumping.
TREVOR. No.
MONA. Hanging.
TREVOR. No.
MONA. Asphyxiation!
TREVOR. No!
MONA. Looking at you?
TREVOR. What?
MONA. Strategically placed Hand gun!
TREVOR. Yeah.

(*Pause.*)

MONA. So you've been with lots of women?
TREVOR. I don't know.
MONA. You ever loved any?
TREVOR. One.
MONA. Why'd you love her?
TREVOR. I still do. Cause of what she's not.
MONA. There's very philosophical, defining somebody by the thing's they're not.
TREVOR. She's an angel.
MONA. You think she's ever done an astronaut?
TREVOR. No.

I think I'd like to go now.
MONA. Excuse me, honey?
TREVOR. Listen, you're rad and all, but I think I'd like to go.
MONA. I can't hear you.

TREVOR. I'd like to go.

MONA. Thanks for helping me carry my groceries.

TREVOR. You're welcome and can I please go?

MONA. YOU WRITE WITH BLUE CHALK! You write with chalk. Trevor, it washes away. I should know. I know this sort of stuff. I have a PHD and an MFA. You're certainly no philosopher.

Your mother probably killed herself because you're stupid.

(*From far away,* **JOANNE**'s *gunshot.* **TREVOR** *jumps.*)

(*She returns to the cocoa. Soft sounds from* **TREVOR** *in the chair, which, ps., faces upstage. She turns back to him.*)

What. *What.* Are you *crying?* Really. He's crying. He's *crying.* I can't – stop it. You want to touch them? (*Sincere*) Please stop crying.

(*She looks at him. She waits. He doesn't stop. Quickly, she unties him. Doesn't look at him.*)

Get out of here. I'm done.

(*He goes off, fast.*)

XII.

(**TREVOR** *sits in the park. He frantically writes a letter. We hear him writing.*)

TREVOR. (*V.O.*) Dear my future wife – I want you to know that I have suddenly definitely decided that there is no one else but you. Everyone else is bad. I have taken the time to look, so that I am sure, I am sorry that I had to do this, I hope this did not make you sad.

But it is definitely you.

For sure, totally, one hundred a million percent.

I love you like a lover should. For real. For real a lot, girl.

So now we have to both run towards God because if two people are running together towards God, eventually he lets them hold hands while they do it. So let's run.

I can't wait to smell your hair forever and teach you how to make me sandwiches. And we're going to make a lot of love, too. I can't wait, Pretty Lady. Your friend. (*Pause.*) Nah. Your HUSBAND, Trevor.

(**TREVOR** *folds the letter neatly and places it inside an envelope, licking it shut. He puts it in his pocket.*)

(**DIANE** *joins him on the bench, elated. She grabs him, hugs him, nuzzles.*)

DIANE. Sorry I'm late!

TREVOR. Nah, it's cool.

DIANE. (*bursting at seams*) So – I have a present for you.

TREVOR. Yeah – I got a surprise for you too!

(She pulls a key out of her pocket and holds it up. With her hurt paw. So this takes a minute, and it's sad.)

TREVOR. It's a key.

DIANE. It's a key to my place. I thought – maybe – we could live – in the same place. All the time.

(TREVOR takes the key and looks at it.)

Um – what do you think?

TREVOR. Wow – it's a pretty cool key!

DIANE. I want you to move in with me.

TREVOR. What?

DIANE. Move in with me.

(Long Pause.)

TREVOR. The thing is.

DIANE. What?

TREVOR. *(with a smile, seriously)* I'm getting married!

(This announcement, this bomb just drop, is happy. TREVOR genuinely is thrilled to share this information with her. He is just that oblivious.)

Yeah, I think I decided to go home and marry that girl! Yeah, I'm getting married.

(Long Pause. TREVOR might start to look at a bird. He then pulls out a joint. JOANNE appears, leaving another message. She is bandaged.)

JOANNE. It's me again. I missed. Not you, I don't miss you, fuck you, I missed myself. It grazed my thigh, I missed, I didn't die. I got thirteen stitches, I'm going to have a scar. It's cute. Want to come over and kiss it? Are you dead? Want to come over and I'll hold you?

(*She disappears.*)

DIANE. Um. Congratulations?

TREVOR. You got a lighter?

> (*Numbly, she hands him one. He lights the joint. He smokes.*)

DIANE. We almost died together.

TREVOR. Yeah, that was pretty cool.

DIANE. When are you going?

TREVOR. Tomorrow.

DIANE. Where you going to tell me?

TREVOR. I'm telling you.

> (*She's not looking at him.*)

I like kissing you.

> (*He tries to kiss her. She moves away.*)

You're not being very cool right now.

DIANE. I, um.

TREVOR. I'm starved.

DIANE. I mean, um. Stay with me. Please stay with me. You won't have to work, I'll pay. You can spend all day, you can do whatever, I'll take care of you, I'll –

TREVOR. Nah. – this girl –

DIANE. ....*Nah?*

TREVOR. I'll miss you, man. (*Pause. He has no idea what to say.*) Good times.

> (*He leaves. Diane, stunned. Tears.* **TREVOR** *comes back.*)

Oh. Hey.

(He holds the letter out to her.)

Could you drop this in a mailbox for me?

(She stares at the letter. Finally, she takes it. She nods.)

Thanks. *(He sees the devastation in her eyes.)* Hey, you'll uh, you'll totally find someone running next to you. You just gotta reach out and grab their hand.

(He kisses her cheek, platonically. He goes. She looks after him. She looks at the envelope. It doesn't have a stamp on it. She sighs. She takes a stamp out of her own wallet, puts it on the letter, and slowly walks off.)

(**GEORGIA** *enters a spot.*)

GEORGIA. There is nothing interesting about your tears.
There is nothing beautiful about them.
Women all over the world
are swallowing back sobs like sandwiches
and remembering how the same sobs felt similar
at ages eight, 12, seventeen, twenty, and twenty one.
The heaves are caused by hormones that
are surging like hurricanes through your body.
They only half happen
because the call didn't come
or because he doesn't love you, or really never did, at all,
or just because it's dark and the bed is as empty
as every year you have yet lived.

(**ANNA** *is playing in the backyard, with her harp. She reads the end of a letter. She lets it drop to the ground.*

TREVOR *appears behind her in a tuxedo. It doesn't fit. He beams with nerves and love. He approaches her. She looks at him. He kneels in front of her. Out of his coat,* *he produces a large red flower. He holds it out to her. It takes her a moment, then she laughs, and laughs, and laughs. This laughing echoes, as –*)

There is nothing poetic about your crying.
It is happening, everywhere.
There is the fact that your eyes get greener when it happens;
there is the fact that you think about funerals, and spit, maybe these specifics are special, but nothing else.
And perhaps the worst part of the whole affair is that
there is nothing interesting about your tears,
and there is nothing beautiful about them.

(*Sparse clapping gradually gains force and turns into full fledge loud claps of appreciation, and lots. Lots and loud, fervor.* **GEORGIA** *lives in this. She grins, bows.*)

Lights.

SET REQUIREMENTS

A brick wall, other than that, open to interpretation!

PROPS

Popsicle (**ANNA**)
Harp (**ANNA**)
Microphone (**GEORGIA**)
Chalk (**TREVOR**)
Skateboard (**TREVOR**)
Walkie Talkie (**DIANE**)
Make-up case (**JOANNE**)
Beer cans (**TREVOR/DIANE**)
Red flower
Flower petals
Tampons (**ANNA**)
Pamprin (**ANNA**)
Cute underwear (**ANNA**)
Strawberry Starbursts (**ANNA**)
Whole bag of just Red Skittles (**ANNA**)
Snack of some sort (**TREVOR**)
A Leaf
Bags of Random Groceries (**MONA**)
Cat food (**MONA**)
Chair (**MONA**)
Rope/ extension chord (**MONA**)
Pen/Pad/Envelope (**TREVOR**)

SOUND EFFECTS

Nature Sounds
City Sounds
Gun Shot
Explosion

www.ingramcontent.com/pod-product-compliance
Lightning Source LLC
Chambersburg PA
CBHW051408290426
44108CB00015B/2207